Between Sea and Sky

Images of Bardsey

BETWEEN SEA AND SKY
Images of Bardsey

Peter Hope Jones
(collation, and photographs of Bardsey)

and

R. S. Thomas
(quotations from poetry)

GOMER

First impression—1998

ISBN 1 85902 483 1

Printed in Wales by
Gomer Press, Llandysul, Ceredigion

THERE IS AN ISLAND THERE IS NO GOING
TO BUT IN A SMALL BOAT THE WAY
THE SAINTS WENT, TRAVELLING THE GALLERY
OF THE FRIGHTENED FACES OF
THE LONG-DROWNED, MUNCHING THE GRAVEL
OF ITS BEACHES

CONTENTS

INTRODUCTION

Bardsey is an island. This simple, but fundamental, fact influences – and often dictates – much of what happens there. It provides opportunities, and it imposes constraints, sometimes in ways which are very obvious, sometimes through a more subtle and nebulous effect which may not be apparent at the time.

This fact of insularity forms a backdrop to the brief description of Bardsey which follows, and to the photographs and quotations. The description and photographs cannot in any of their aspects or images be comprehensive, but I hope they will help create for the reader a sense of place. I hope they will give – to those who have visited Bardsey – a sweet aftertaste, and a keen anticipation of future visits; and I hope they will encourage – in those who have not yet visited – an interest in, and a sympathy for, this marvellous island which so many people have come to love and cherish.

THE ISLAND

Physical images

Bardsey lies 4 km off the tip of the Llŷn peninsula in Gwynedd. It comprises 178 ha of land in a larger northern portion of lowland and 'mountain' (1.5 km by 1 km), and a smaller southern peninsula (1 km by 0.5 km). The two are separated by a neck of land only some 30 m across at its narrowest point.

Geologically, Bardsey belongs mainly in the Precambrian era (over 600 million years ago) with some later additions and intrusions. Scarred by glaciers – which eventually deposited the dross which would evolve into the island's soil – it emerged into its present form about 8,000 years ago when sea-levels stabilised. Ever since, it has been subject to those effects of sea, rain, wind and temperature which together create the present temperate maritime environment.

The physical image presented by Bardsey is janus-like: facing the mainland is the stern, craggy, unpromising aspect, whilst beyond (and visible only from the island itself or the adjacent sea) lie the softer, more amenable, slopes and lowlands of the island facing west and south.

Historical images

Evidence for prehistoric occupation verges on the non-existent (some earth circles on the mountain have been ascribed to Bronze Age construction) and the first peoples with some 'real' history are the religious. Christianity, of various subspecies, played a role in shaping the island's history from the sixth century (Celtic Church) to the twelfth (Augustinians), to the nineteenth (Calvinistic Methodists) to the late twentieth (interdenominational).

The settlement axis lies along the break of slope between the mountain and the more manageable lowland, with the remains of the Augustinian abbey tower dominating the buildings at the northern end.

The Middle Ages saw a mixture of religious occupation with presumably the start of the farming and fishing community system which was eventually to predominate. Ownership was vested in large estates on the adjacent peninsula (Bodfel, 1549-1752;

11

Glynllifon, 1752-1972), and apart from an era of piracy and associated skullduggery in the sixteenth and seventeenth centuries, the tenants managed the island on the basis mainly of common grazing on the mountain and mixed farming of hay, rough grazing, corn, roots and pulses in small fields in the more agriculturally-tractable lowland. Fishing was always a concomitant source of food and, latterly, of revenue.

The lighthouse was constructed, mainly of imported limestone, in 1821, and a major house-building programme, carried out to the instructions of Sir Spencer Bulkeley Wynn, 3rd Lord Newborough, was completed in the period 1875-1900, producing the present fine show of houses, outbuildings and chapel.

With its population declining to one resident farming family, the island was sold to a private owner in 1972, then acquired by the Bardsey Island Trust in 1979.

Bardsey's historical image is similar to that of several western islands: a shadowy prehistory; early and continuing religiosity; racy piracy; tenant farming coupled with fishing; and finally (at least so far) an acquisition and designation where nature conservation plays a major role in a multiple-use management.

Wildlife images

Its farming history dictates that probably extremely little of the land surface of Bardsey remains uninfluenced by the activities of humans and their agricultural stock. Despite this (and, in certain instances, because of this) the wildlife of the island is of sufficient importance to have warranted its designation as a Site of Special Scientific Interest in 1953, and its creation as a National Nature Reserve in 1986. It is currently managed by the Bardsey Island Trust, with help and advice from the Countryside Council for Wales.

Of special importance, interest and value are: the whole marine and littoral ecosystems surrounding the island; some major terrestrial habitats such as maritime grasslands and heaths; and a range of species which include Grey Seal, Chough, Manx Shearwater, and several lichens and flowering plants.

The known impressive movements of migratory birds through the island prompted the creation of the Bardsey Bird and Field Observatory in 1953. Based at Cristin, one of Lord Newborough's houses of the late nineteenth century, the Observatory has collected records on many aspects of the island's natural history, and it continues to foster interest in that field, to discover new features, and to publish its findings in an annual Report.

The abiding image of Bardsey's wildlife is of tenacity and flexibility in the face of long human exploitation of land and sea: doubtless much of the 'original' flora and fauna has been lost, but the remaining diversity is still well worth conserving and studying as the basis for a continuing conservation management project in which wildlife figures prominently.

Cultural images

Unlike certain islands such as, for example, the Blaskets in western Ireland, Bardsey did not spawn a series of writers who would document their island's mores. Certainly, there are reports, articles, booklets and books even, which give us tantalising glimpses of life on the island at certain periods but a coherent social history has yet to be produced. These and other documents contain statements or whole sections with research results, true anecdotes, fabulous tales, myths and downright idiocies, so that a seeker after objective reporting despairs of ever arriving at anything approaching a factual appraisal. Taken with distinctly more than the proverbial pinch of salt, the accrued literature makes fascinating reading, but let the reader beware.

Picking over this medley of fact and fantasy one learns that there was at least one eisteddfod (festival of song, poetry and literature), there were three consecutive 'kings' of the island confirmed in office by a tin crown made at the behest of Lord Newborough; and there was a café at Tŷ Pellaf catering for the sustenance of numerous day-visitors coming – in the balmier weather of the 1930s – from as far away as Caernarfon and Aberystwyth.

There have been at least two major changes in communities, so that finding a long lineage of Bardsey families is not a likely proposition; the census returns indicate an island population rising from 70 in 1811, peaking at about 90 in mid-nineteenth century, and dropping drastically to four by 1993.

The island has done reasonably well by artists, receiving attention from Moses Griffiths (Pennant's illustrator in the late eighteenth century), Brenda Chamberlain (1940s and 1950s), Cicely Williams-Ellis (1950s-1980s) and Kim Atkinson (1980s-1990s).

Welsh was the island residents' language from some ill-defined start until 1970. It is now re-emerging from a partial eclipse and is to be heard regularly amongst some residents and visitors, and is accorded due equality with English in documents such as the Bardsey Trust's Newsletter.

Bardsey's cultural image is a disappointment. In a field where so much is dependent on transmission to succeeding generations, written and oral traditions are few, and we can only hope that the Bardsey Island Trust takes serious note of its avowed intents to encourage research into the history of the island, and to promote publication and dissemination of results.

Better late than never.

Metaphysical images

As would be expected of an island off the western coast of Europe, the prevailing theism over the centuries has been Christianity. In the Middle Ages, Bardsey acquired an aura of sanctity which led to its acceptance as the terminus of major pilgrim routes across north-western Wales – an eminent position which doubtless helped swell the coffers of the local religious communities, as well as providing the requisite religious satisfaction for the pilgrims. In the eighteenth, nineteenth and early twentieth centuries, the dank shroud of Calvinism enveloped the island, but in recent years, the brighter hopes and philosophies of an interdenominational usage have made the chapel into a place of encouraging accord between potentially antagonistic Christian factors.

Bardsey's Christian sanctity has so dominated the island's culture and history that only in recent decades has there emerged an overt acceptance of the island's spiritual or philosophical value separate from a theistic interpretation. Many visitors comment on the peace and quiet which the island affords as an antidote to the noisy pace of mainland life; some can extend this comforting feeling into realms of meditation and contemplation. Bardsey certainly acts as a catalyst for many disparate human thoughts, feelings and aspirations, such that the final product becomes a pleasing and fulfilling revelation for the recipient.

A third, shadowy, parallel-world aspect of metaphysics (in some ways analogous to the anti-matter theories of modern cosmology) comprises those myths and fabulous tales, based on truth or half-truth coupled with vivid imagination, which seem deeply satisfying to so many human cultures. Bardsey epitomises the 'island in the west' so beloved of mediaeval romancers, and it is not surprising that it has been accorded the status of Merlin's last resting place and Arthur's Avalon: a site for rest and recovery after his injury in the Battle of Camlan.

The whole image

I sense that people approach Bardsey initially through facets of an image: say birds, or geology, or history, or religious retreat, or just 'peace and quiet'. It is only after some time that those open to such development can begin to appreciate how their initial entry point forms just part of a fascinating whole.

Partial images of Bardsey can be seen in most of the pools at various places round the island: bright and transparent (as in intertidal pools near Maen Du); clear but ephemeral (as in occasional rainwater pools at Pencafn); artificial but useful (as in the dammed Pwll Cain); deep and clear or shallow and muddy (as in some of the island's wells). None of these forms a complete image of Bardsey either literally or metaphorically, but all contribute towards that elusive whole image, and each illustrates a facet which is true in its own time and place.

It is well-nigh impossible for any one individual to grasp and assimilate this whole image, but this is one of the features which makes Bardsey such a fascinating topic – it becomes a concept rather than a collection of bald facts and, in R.S.'s words, it is an island 'that we had found and would spend the rest of our lives looking for'.

Luckily, many facets of the Bardsey whole are accessible to most people without the need for arcane search methods. The whole image is surely so much more than the sum of its facetted parts, and whilst this grail-like whole image is well worth striving after, even if unattainable, the island can still provide a wide range of interest, experience and image for all who are interested. The preservation of just one image of the island is neither feasible nor necessary, and images of Bardsey will continue to evolve – as life itself is evolving; sympathetic and beneficent management will ensure a gentle evolution for the island and an increasingly rich store of images.

Evolution of this book

In 1984 and 1985 I was lucky enough to spend two summers on Bardsey – an island which has entranced me since my first visit there in the late 1950s. One of my main aims was to organise an archive of photographs to record the 'state' of Bardsey in the mid-1980s and to attempt subsequently an annual recording of changes – in habitat, land use, general appearance, wildlife, islanders and their activities – so that people in the twenty-first century could see how Bardsey was in the 1980s and 1990s and how it was changing.

Among these purely 'record' photographs, it was impossible not to include some which showed more than just the surface elements and superficial changes. And some effort was also made to show specifically what Bardsey meant to me: not just the obvious elements of its present appearance and wildlife, but some deeper appreciation of those feelings engendered by the island's history, sanctity, weather and Celtic ambience.

To a photographer, the light on Bardsey has special elements and reverberations, so that it seems possible to indicate – through the medium of a particular photograph – rather more than the scene shows at face value. The juxtaposition of selected photographs with some of R.S.'s poetry seemed to offer an opportunity for extending the value of the photographs even further, so that the viewer could perhaps gain synergistic value from the two art forms – enjoying the use of light in creating the photographic image, and enjoying the use of words in creating the poetic image, then further, in some cases using the combination of the two images to form a wholly new creation.

I hope that the idea works, and I hope that the visitor to Bardsey and the disinterested viewer will gain some extra insight into the beauty of word and light which this volume invites.

Grey waters, vast
  as an area of prayer
that one enters.

The running of the sea under the wind,
Rough with silver, comes before my mind

And they come sailing
From the island through the flocks
Of the sea with the boat full
Of their own flocks

With
what relish a kitten converts
its tail into a serpent?

From what was I escaping?
There is a rare peace here.

shadows advance
From their corners to take possession
Of places the light held
For an hour

Both window and mirror

From meditation on a flower
you think more flowers will be born
of your mind?

the white accompaniment of the sea's laughter.

I listen;
they are far off,
the echoes return slow.

the grey
Traffic of the clouds going by

I return to Lleyn
repository of the condescension
of time.

At some stage
in the crossing of it a traveller
rejoiced.

Nature had invested all her gold
In the industry of the soil.

In Wales there are jewels
To gather, but with the eye
Only.

27

I have looked long at this land,
Trying to understand
My place in it

cold sea, cold sky

and this was a civilisation
that came to nothing

It is beautiful and still;
   the air rarified
as the interior of a cathedral
expecting a presence.

and the October day
Burns slowly down.

There are places, where you might have been sent
To learn patience

I have seen the sun break through
to illuminate a small field
for a while, and gone my way
and forgotten it. But that was the pearl
of great price, the one field that had
the treasure in it.

It was arranged so:
An impression of nearness
contradicted by blank space.

33

Who bothers
    where this road goes?
It is not for getting people
    anywhere, at least
not at speed.

And the world will grow to a few lean acres of grass

The stone in Llŷn
is still there, honey-
coloured for a girl's hair
to resemble.

Here I think of the centuries,
Six million of them, they say.

If he had not given them stone
how could they have begun building?

Here
by the sea they said little.
But their message to the future
was: Build well.

There is peace there of a kind,
  Though not the deep peace
of wild places.

Here there is no sleep
for the dead, they are resurrected
to mourn. Everywhere is the sad
chorus of an old people, waking to weep.

The sand crumbles
like bread; the wine is
the light quietly lying
in its own chalice.

The salt current swings in and out
of the bay, as it has done
time out of mind. How does that help?
It leaves illegible writing
on the shore.

You have to imagine
a waiting game that is not impatient
because it is timeless

After the dark
The dawning
After the first light
The sun.
After the calm the wind
Creasing the water

Not darkness but twilight
in which even the best
of minds must make its way
now.

And God said, I will build a church here
And cause this people to worship me,
And afflict them with poverty and sickness
In return for centuries of hard work
And patience.

the staid chapel, where the Book's frown
Sobers the sunlight

Moments of great calm,
Kneeling before an altar
Of wood in a stone church
In summer, waiting for the God
To speak; the air a staircase
For silence; the sun's light
Ringing me, as though I acted
A great role.

43

It was not his first time to be crucified.

I looked out on a grey world,
grey with despair.

In our country you make your way
from monument to monument.

It was a bare
landscape and harsh, and geological
its time. But the rock was
bright, the illuminated manuscript
of the lichen.

Everywhere pattern;
design without a designer?
I gather a bird's feather
which looks at me in
silence and tells all.

Sometimes a shadow passed
between him and the light.

There is no present in Wales,
And no future;
There is only the past,
Brittle with relics,
Wind-bitten towers and castles

These grey skies, these wet fields,
With the wind's winding-sheet upon them

One particular
time after a harsh morning
of rain, the clouds lifted, the wind
fell; there was a resurrection
of nature, and we there to emerge
with it into the annointed
air.

49

Here was the marriage
of land and sea, from whose bickering
the spray rises.

What is existence
but standing patiently for a while
amid flux?

You cannot live in the present,
At least not in Wales.

It was beautiful as God
must be beautiful

What is water
but mirror, air but returner
of the personal cadenza

53

And in the foreground
The tall Cross,
Sombre, untenanted
Aches for the Body.

No longer the Lamb
but the idea of it

A promontory is a bare
place; no God leans down
out of the air to take the hand
extended to him. The generations have
watched there
in vain.

There is a rock pointing
in no direction but its ability
to hold hard.

On an evening like this
the furies have receded

the tranquility that inheres
before thought, or the purity of thought
without language

Your move I would have
said, but he was not
playing; my game a dilemma
that was without horns.

But behind the flower
is that other flower
which is ageless, the idea
of the flower

You know what flowers
do best on. I think how the bodies
of the centuries have been rendered down
that this one should emerge, innocent of
compassion.

There was something I was near
and never attained: a pattern
an explanation.

It is such a small thing,
Easily overlooked in the multitude
Of the worlds.

The farmer changed his allegiance from
Ceres to Mars, from subsistence to profit.

They made the grey stone
Blossom, setting it on a branch
Of the wind; airy cathedrals
Grew

Awry like an old thorn for lack
of the soil's depth

And destitute as a tree stripped
Of foliage under a bald sky.

Spring's bloom is spent,
Summer is done, too.

The sky's ruins, gutted with fire
Of the late sun, smouldering still

There is no time on this island.
The swinging pendulum of the tide
has no clock; the events
are dateless.

Who is skilled to read
The strange epitaph of the salt wind
Scrawled on our shores?

Richness is in the ability
of poverty to conceal itself

the hole under the door
Was a mouth through which the rough wind spoke
Ever more sharply

Island Boatman

That they should be braille
to him on blind days
of fog or of drizzle
he learned them by heart,
murmuring them over:
Pen Cristin, Briw Gerrig,
Ogof y Morlas. I listened
to them and they were music
of a marine world
where everybody wore ermine.

Was he religious?
He was member of an old
congregation the white-
surpliced island ministered

to, warning of the crossing
to a smiling Aberdaron
with tides at the spring.

Sitting with him over
a fire of salt wood,
spitting and purring, I
forgave him his clichés,
his attempt to live up
to his eyes' knowingness.
They had looked down so many
times without flinching
into a glass coffin
at the shipwreck of such
bones as might have been his.

The castle was
huge. All that dead weight
of the past.

The wind was high,
   and savage swung the tide

It is not your light that
can blind us; it is the splendour
of your darkness.

I look up from my book,
from the unreality of language,
and stare at the sea's surface
that says nothing and means it.

listening
to the swell born somewhere in the Atlantic
rising and falling, rising and falling
wave on wave on the long shore

Simple in your designs,
infinite in your variations
upon them

History goes on,
On the rock the lichen
Records it: no mention
Of them, of us.

I have crawled out at last
far as I dare on to a bough
of country that is suspended
between sky and sea.

                                        a nice place
                                  Of bracken, a looking-glass
                                  For the sea that not far off
                                  Glitters.

So beautiful it hurts;
yet nothing for tears
to exploit

Out of the soil the buds come,
The silent detonations
Of power wielded without sin

Silent silver sea
Reflecting waves of longing.
Sorrowful island.

The monks would be proud:
Despite the passage of time
Their faith rings out still.

End of one big storm.
'The furies have receded';
Wait – there's more to come.

Redundant gatepost,
Shipwrecked in a bracken sea.
Useless, but still proud.

APPENDIX 1

Colour photographs

(front cover) Bardsey from Uwchmynydd, February.

(back cover) Bardsey from Uwchmynydd, dusk, December. Welsh landscape.

(frontispiece) The Newborough cross, September.

(page 6) Carline thistles on the mountain, October.

Page	*Description*
17	Looking south-east from the mountain, April. Sea-watching; Hiraeth.
22	Flowering Thrift on a coastal field wall, June. The echoes return slow.
26	Llŷn across the Bardsey Sound, June. The earth does its best for him; Travellers.
27	Wild Thyme on the mountain, July. The small window; A line from St. David's.
31	Dead Foxglove at dusk, October. Moorland; Autumn on the land.
32	Fields below the trackway, September. Country cures; The bright field.
36	Shore rocks in the bay Solfach, September. Pen Llŷn; Pre-Cambrian.
37	The mountain wall, June. Sarn Rhiw; B.C.
40	Seawater pool at low tide, September. In great waters; Correspondence.
41	South-east coast, early morning, September. p. 81 in *The echoes return slow*; Becoming.
42	Chapel roof, late afternoon, September. The answer; The island.
43	Pulpit and altar table in the chapel, September. Kneeling; Chapel deacon.
47	Feather on lichened rock near lighthouse, October. The film of God; The seasons: summer.
48	Abbey tower wall at sunset, September. This one; Welsh landscape.
49	Towards the south end on a wet day, September. That; One place.
50	Sea breaking on rocks, October. Pen Llŷn; Afon Rhiw.
54	Cross in graveyard, September. Pieta; Agnus Dei.
55	Maen Du, Bardsey's southernmost point, April. Emerging; p. 87 in *The echoes return slow.*
56	Across the bay – Solfach at sunset, September. The un-born; A.D.
58	Flowerhead of Autumn Hawkbit, October. Flowers; p. 23 in *The echoes return slow.*
59	Snail in dewy vegetation on a field wall, March. Sonata in X; Earth.
62	Wind-blasted dead Hawthorn, June. Priest and peasant; An old man.
63	Nettles at sunset, August. Harvest end; Hireling.
64	Thongweed thrown up by tide, September. Pilgrimages; The question.

Black and white

Page	Description
53	'Benlli' on its cradle at Pencafn. BC (p. 18).
57	One of the island rams. Play.
60	Sheep in 'holding fields' after a round-up; p. 28 of *The echoes return slow*.
61	Lighthouse tower. Art history.
67	Lichened walls of the ruined abbey tower. To pay for his keep.
68	Seafoam on coast during westerly gale. Night and morning.
69	Moon above the lighthouse on a clear evening. Shadows.
73	Icelandic Merlin caught for ringing at the Observatory. Pissaro: the Louveciennes road.
74	Flower spike of Autumn Lady's-tresses orchid. The garden.

APPENDIX 2

Publishing details for each volume quoted, with the titles of those poems from which the quotations are derived.

The stones of the field, Druid Press, Carmarthen, 1946.
    The question; Country child; Night and morning; Hiraeth.
An acre of land, Montgomeryshire Printing Co., Newtown, 1952.
    Depopulation of the hills; Welsh landscape.
The minister, Montgomeryshire Printing Co., Newtown, 1953.
Song at the year's turning, Hart-Davis, London, 1955.
    Autumn on the land; Priest and peasant.
Poetry for supper, Hart-Davis, London, 1958.
    Chapel deacon.
Tares, Hart-Davis, London, 1961.
    An old man; Hireling; Those others; Hyddgen.
The bread of truth, Hart-Davis, London, 1963.
    A line from St. David's; Country cures; Becoming; The garden; The untamed.
Pieta, Hart-Davis, London, 1966.
    Pieta; Gospel truth; In church.
Not that he brought flowers, Hart-Davis, London, 1968.
    The observer; Kneeling; Art history; The small window; That.
H'm, Macmillan, London, 1972.
    Ruins; The island; Repeat; Earth.

Young and old, Chatto & Windus, London, 1972.
   Young and old; Islandmen.
What is a Welshman? Christopher Davies, Llandybie, 1974.
   To pay for his keep; He lies down to be counted; The earth does its best for him.
Laboratories of the spirit, Macmillan, London, 1975.
   Welsh summer; One place; The bright field; Sea-watching.
The way of it, Ceolfrith, Sunderland, 1977.
   Travellers.
Frequencies, Macmillan, London, 1978.
   Shadows; Pre-Cambrian; Pilgrimages; The film of God; The answer; The white tiger; Emerging; In great waters; Henry James; Play.
Between here and now, Macmillan, London, 1981.
   Flowers; Correspondence; Monet: The Bas-Bréau road; Pissaro: the Louveciennes road.
Ingrowing thoughts, Poetry Wales Press, Bridgend, 1985.
   Drawing by a child: Diana Brinton Lee.
Experimenting with an amen, Macmillan, London, 1986.
   Cones; Harvest end; Sarn Rhiw; Retirement; Moorland; This one.
Three poems, Words Press, Dorset, 1988.
   The un-born.
The echoes return slow, Macmillan, London, 1988.
   pages 23, 63, 79, 81, 87; page 28 (prose), page 72 (prose).
Counterpoint, Bloodaxe, Newcastle upon Tyne, 1990.
   B.C. (pages 16 and 18); A.D. (pages 48 and 57).
Mass for hard times, Bloodaxe, Newcastle upon Tyne, 1992.
   Agnus Dei; The seasons: summer; Pen Llŷn; The letter; Afon Rhiw; Sonata in X.

Acknowledgements

We are very grateful to Helen Roberts and Dr. Gareth Wyn Jones for early help towards publication. The Council of the Bardsey Island Trust was very supportive of the project; and many Bardsey residents past and present, especially Jane and Arthur Strick, were helpful in kindly allowing PHJ to photograph them or their stock and crops. Finally, we wish to acknowledge, with thanks, the kind and professional help of Dyfed Elis-Gruffydd of Gwasg Gomer in guiding the project through its numerous stages.